Communication

A Comprehensive Manual For Enhancing Your
Interpersonal Acumen, Oratory Skills, And Verbal
Communication In Social Contexts

*(Enhance Your Interpersonal Abilities And Refine Your
Conversational Skills)*

Annette Fay

TABLE OF CONTENT

The Fundamentals Of Communication 1

Share Your Own Stories 8

Persuasive Discourse In The Era Of Digital Technology 29

Relationship And Mirroring 41

Specific Scenarios For Cultivating Empathetic Communication 54

Overcoming Unfavorable Habits 72

People-Pleasing 104

The Body Language Of Gender 118

Four Practical Recommendations For Effective Communication Across Various Platforms ... 125

Mimes Explain My Feelings 129

Communication - An Innate Human Instinct 135

Mastering The Art Of Workplace Communication 141

Implementing Visual Approaches For Environmental Organization 152

The Fundamentals Of Communication

Could you envision the extent of disarray our lives would descend into in the absence of effective communication? How can peace or unity be attained in its absence? How would you be able to successfully complete even the most basic projects if the individuals involved lacked the ability to comprehend one another? That's how important communication is – our lives would be unrecognizable without it!

At this juncture, I trust that I have sufficiently impressed upon you the significance of communication and the utmost necessity for you to become a proficient communicator. However, prior to delving into the specifics, allow me to elucidate the mechanics of a straightforward communication process. Gaining knowledge of the communication process will enable you to gain a deeper comprehension of the specific elements within the process that necessitate improvement on your part.

The process of communication

There are numerous processes and theories that elucidate interpersonal communication; however, at its most basic level, it encompasses seven essential elements: the sender, the encoding of the message, the communication channel or medium, the presence of external disruptions or noise, the decoding of the message, the receiver, and the provision of feedback.

The originator of the communication is the individual who commences the interaction by transmitting a message. Initially, it is necessary for him to convert or encode his cogitations into a comprehensible medium such as verbal or written language.

The term "message channel" pertains to the medium through which a message is transmitted. Messages can be conveyed via various channels including verbal communication, written language, tactile interaction, electronic mail, and even nonverbal cues.

To facilitate communication with the recipient, it is necessary to decipher or construe the message beforehand, ensuring the intended recipient comprehends the message being conveyed by the sender. Effective communication necessitates appropriate encoding and decoding for the communication process to achieve its intended outcome. Noise encompasses various elements that impede the precise transmission of information.

Upon successful delivery of the sender's message, the recipient will then provide feedback in response to the sender's communication.

Categories of Communication

The primary objective of this literary work is to facilitate the enhancement of your proficiency in communicating effectively. In order to accomplish this, it is imperative that one attains proficiency in three forms of communication.

Verbal Communication

Verbal communication, commonly referred to as oral communication, employs the use of spoken language as a means of transmitting information. There are various modes of verbal communication apart from direct interpersonal interaction, encompassing telephone conversations, deliberations in the workplace, video conferences, and even public speaking engagements. In order to enhance your oral communication abilities, it is imperative to cultivate your aptitude for active listening and articulate expression.

Non-Verbal Communication

Non-verbal communication encompasses the transmission of thoughts and emotions through means other than spoken language. In order to attain proficiency in this form of communication, one must nurture their capacity to decipher body language, facial expressions, posture, and gestures – commonly referred to as physical non-verbal communication.

An alternative manner to express the same idea in a formal tone: "An additional variant of non-verbal communication can be identified as paralanguage, encompassing the deciphering of information derived from the manner in which a message is delivered." Instances of paralanguage encompass elements such as intonation, tonality, pitch variations, and vocal characteristics.

Additional types of non-verbal communication encompass aesthetic communication, encompassing art forms such as painting and dancing; spatial language, encompassing indicators of a person's status or taste; symbols, which serve as icons for conveying information; and appearance, pertaining to the manner in which an individual expresses their personality.

Written Communication

This third form of communication holds great significance for professionals and individuals pursuing their careers, although it can be universally beneficial as written communication enables the expression of intricate concepts through the written medium. This form of communication is employed for purposes such as submitting reports, sending emails to superiors, or composing proposals for new projects. However, it is also utilized when transmitting text messages or writing letters.

In order to excel in this form of communication, it is imperative to cultivate and refine your writing abilities. To enhance your proficiency in writing, endeavor to cultivate a robust comprehension of prevalent grammatical, spelling, and punctuation inaccuracies and endeavor to render your writing coherent and succinct.

Do not fret if you were not born with the innate aptitude for writing. The art of writing, akin to any other form of communication, can be acquired through diligent practice.

Share Your Own Stories

Numerous live performers or speakers possess the ability to effectively communicate and present their material with sincerity.

It requires a distinct set of abilities to articulate a personal anecdote in a manner akin to conversing with a close acquaintance or relative, yet this can yield significant outcomes. The individuals who display the highest level of efficacy in captivating their audience regularly demonstrate a deliberate inclination towards disclosing the underlying narrative behind their presentation, elucidating the significance that the content holds for them.

For poets or singer-songwriters, the act of recounting narratives or tales can furnish the listeners with insights that imbue an additional stratum of significance and profundity to a previously cherished poem or song, whose true essence might have eluded their comprehension. Additionally, it has the potential to imbue a certain warmth and human connection into their initial encounter with the material, consequently increasing the likelihood of their undivided attention and sincere comprehension, rather than merely engaging in passive actions such as flipping through pages or adjusting their guitar strings in silence.

Alternatively, failing to address this issue may result in a significantly larger portion of the audience being prone to diverting their attention towards their mobile devices, engaging in social media, or engaging in conversations with one another. I once attended a live performance in Kentish Town, London, wherein a musical group commenced their concluding piece without providing verbal introductory remarks. Adjacent to my location, a young lady remained stationary, engaging in the act of perusing a literary work using the illumination provided by a handheld light source. Remarkably, upon the commencement of this particular piece of music, the aforementioned individual did not divert her attention from the printed pages nor display any discernible response.

Stand-up comedians tend to achieve heightened effectiveness by employing extensive anecdotes rooted in personal experiences, rather than merely presenting an incessant flow of one-liners. The restrained use of concise remarks can be advantageous, yet an excessive dependence on them may lead to the performer's act seeming contrived, excessively polished, or superficial.

Motivational speakers tend to be particularly impactful when they recount their own personal narratives of overcoming adversity, commonly known as "rags to riches" tales (and I do not solely imply financial prosperity). This stands in opposition to individuals who merely propagate statements without substantiating their credibility or providing a rationale for accepting the information they present. In the absence of anecdotal evidence, the audience may ponder, "While this information is commendable, what assurance do I have regarding its efficacy?"

When individuals narrate their personal experiences, it enhances the efficacy of their advice and increases the audience's motivation to heed it. In addition, providing an avenue for the audience to participate by raising their hands and offering comments can foster a stronger inclination for them to share their own pertinent experiences.

Adopt the principle of treating others in the same manner that you yourself desire to be treated.

Consider it from this perspective: you engage in the act of enjoying a cup of coffee with either a friend, family member, or romantic partner. What would be your reaction upon observing their persistent restlessness and tendency to divert their gaze towards the ceiling or the floor throughout most of the conversation, while exhibiting minimal engagement through eye contact, smiles, and facial expressions?

Distant?

Alienated?

Maybe even under-valued.

The aforementioned principle remains applicable when addressing sizable audiences as it does when engaging in one-on-one dialogue.

It is crucial to avoid giving the impression that you disregarded the presence of the audience or preferred being somewhere else.

It is generally advisable to refrain from merely reciting and conveying the information word-for-word without actively involving the audience. By exerting deliberate intention to communicate spontaneously, you will enhance your immediate engagement, rather than merely regarding the act as a practice session executed before an audience.

Impromptu speaking can present a significant challenge to individuals who are unfamiliar with it, and I certainly found myself in such a predicament. One possible alternative in a formal tone: "In order to acknowledge the repetition of certain material that has been previously witnessed by the compère or specific audience members, it would be appropriate to engage in a playful apology, humorously recognizing the potential tedium caused by the recurrent performance."

One could discuss the slippery nature of the stage and express the intent to have worn footwear with enhanced traction, had prior knowledge about this characteristic been available.

In broad terms, it is advisable to maintain a jovial disposition when offering observations and remarks.

Exerting oneself to establish eye contact, even if infrequently while briefly diverting attention from a document or a task, appears to be an uncomplicated notion. While I aim to avoid stating the obvious, it is truly astounding how few individuals adhere to this practice.

Certain individuals may perceive establishing eye contact with the audience as intimidating or unsettling, particularly if they are not accustomed to it. However, with regular practice and increased familiarity in addressing crowds, this task can gradually become less challenging. Individuals who consistently endeavor to overcome this obstacle, even if it requires progressing gradually, shall experience the benefits and establish stronger rapport with any observers present.

It is not obligatory to deliver a complete lecture or performance without the use of a microphone. It may not be recommended for individuals experiencing medical conditions affecting their vocal abilities or those who lack sufficient vocal training and frequently engage in silent activities for extended durations. Nevertheless, should it be possible to accomplish this for individual words or phrases, it can undeniably captivate and engross the audience. It holds the potential to emanate a more authentic demeanor, thus fostering in the audience a deeper sense of a natural and sincere bond with the orator.

Significant differentiation is not observed between exhibiting confidence in one's abilities and displaying arrogance. Individuals with excessively inflated egos tend to elicit unfavorable reactions from audiences, and the same would apply to you.

Audience participation

The relationship between the speaker and the audience is consistently reciprocal. Nevertheless, it is incumbent upon you, as the speaker, to initiate the proceedings.

Incorporating your audience into the process to a limited extent can serve to alleviate your anxiety and reduce your sense of solitude, while providing them with a similar effect.

In the context of delivering a lighthearted presentation or stand-up comedy routine centered around your past encounters in the retail or catering industry, you may consider inviting the audience to raise their hands if they too have prior experience in this occupational domain.

One feasible approach would involve posing a sequence of inquiries to the audience, affording them the opportunity to raise their hands and endeavor to provide you with the desired responses.

In a similar vein, you could approach this matter from a different perspective by devoting a portion of your allocated speaking time to entertaining inquiries from the attendees.

Question-and-answer sessions hold significance, as they provide the audience with an opportunity to seek clarification on previously discussed matters or raise pertinent issues that have not been addressed thus far. By means of this approach, the orator can demonstrate to the audience that their perspectives and judgments are highly regarded, and that the act of attentively hearing them out and striving to comprehend their standpoint is of utmost importance.

Likewise, affording the audience an opportunity to participate in a vote concerning a topic pertaining to the presentation or the event at large can yield considerable efficacy (and may occasionally be endowed with an enjoyable essence).

The speaker might also extend an invitation to individuals from the audience to join them on the stage (or similar designated space) in order to assist with a demonstration.

Display your emotions openly

It is not obligatory to disclose deeply personal experiences or emotions that could potentially cause discomfort or distress when shared. Undoubtedly, it would be deemed inappropriate and unlikely to yield any advantages.

This principle also does not encompass the act of divulging every intricate aspect of one's life to the audience, thus avoiding the risk of inundating them with superfluous information.

Nevertheless, on certain occasions during my presentations, I have unintentionally articulated my ideas in a manner that differed from my previous expressions.

The act of openly displaying one's emotions is not synonymous with simply trying to appear genuine, warm, and sincere. Rather, it entails genuinely embodying those qualities of authenticity, warmth, and sincerity.

Naturally, should a presenter illustrate stories or provide information that is concocted, attendees are likely to harbor doubts, potentially leading to a sense of detachment or diminished interest in their credibility and message.

Do not excessively prioritize your own self-importance

Frequently, the audience tends to unwind if as a speaker, you refrain from being excessively serious and instead, maintain a lighthearted demeanor, even when discussing grave matters. It must be noted that making light of distressing situations occurring globally or behaving in an inappropriate manner is strongly discouraged.

Nonetheless, it is crucial to retain the attention of individuals in the audience who might be inclined to disengage if a consistently solemn tone is maintained throughout your presentation.

Narrating an anecdote concerning a humiliating error committed by oneself can serve as a highly effective conversation starter, given that it pertains to the overarching objective and underlying content of one's discourse, just as humorously remarking upon resemblances to notable public figures can accomplish the same outcome.

By the same token, it is important to get the balance right, and not to spill over too much into self-deprecation.

The attendees are not inclined to listen to a presenter who consistently engages in self-deprecating remarks. The audience anticipates the speaker to possess a specific level of self-assurance and expertise when addressing the subject matter, notwithstanding any inherent lack of overall confidence in public speaking. However, should they master the craft of downplaying their experiences or subject matter in a jovial manner on occasion, it is plausible that the audience will experience a reduced sense of detachment.

HIGH PRIESTESS TAROT

Should you identify with the High Priestess archetype, it is imperative that you remain vigilant in ensuring that you do not detach yourself from the fabric of existence and the bonds of your interpersonal connections. Expand beyond the constraints that hinder your progress, as they are solely a product of your own cognition. Do you frequently experience feelings of sadness or low mood? Begin dedicating a greater portion of yourself to nurturing your significant connections and refrain from evading emotional commitment when situations escalate in significance. Permit the natural course of your life to unfold. Existence was not intended to be filled with arduous trials, and your presence on this planet does not signify your obligation to detach from others.

Allow individuals and experiences to enter.

If you are currently engaged in a romantic relationship or dating someone whom you perceive as your twin flame, symbolizing the archetype of the High Priestess, it is plausible that you may experience a sense of unfamiliarity towards this individual.

The individual known as your twin flame possesses an inclination to appear and depart at their own discretion, displaying a perceptibly differing perspective towards life from your own. On certain occasions, one may experience a sense of progress within the relationship. You experience a deep sense of connection with your twin flame, who has recently bestowed upon you a profound encounter with genuine intimacy. Subsequently, you both become unfamiliar to one another once more. The cycle perpetuates in a recurring manner.

In the event that the presence of the High Priestess is observed in your love reading, it indicates the existence of a telepathic bond between you and your twin flame.

This represents an intensity of affection that may resemble a state of interdependence.

One experiences a profound connection with their twin flame, perceiving their thoughts and emotions, and harboring a deep longing for one another. However, despite this bond, the relationship does not progress into a committed state.

In the context of a love tarot reading, the High Priestess may suggest a profound form of intuition and subconscious shifts in one's emotional condition that border on a telepathic nature. The High Priestess indicates the necessity of exercising patience and relying on your innate perception and intuition. Within a romantic partnership, the presence of the High Priestess card signifies a notable elevation in emotional connectedness and vulnerability over the course of twelve stages.

your twin flame.

13

TAROT CARD: THE MONARCH OF CHALICES

The King of Cups represents a favorable indication, particularly for women seeking a long-term commitment with their ideal partner – be it their twin flame or soulmate. It is uncommon for the King of Cups to be without a spouse or to actively seek a committed partnership. He enjoys the company of others; nurturing a loving family holds great significance in his life.

The King of Cups implies that it would be worthwhile to acknowledge the warning signs from previous relationships in which you tended to select partners who were primarily focused on themselves and lacked a genuine understanding of your desires. In the near future, you are likely to break away from this cycle of behavior.

If one happens to be unmarried or going through a period of separation, it can be regarded as highly advantageous to observe the appearance of the King of Cups in one's Tarot reading. Based on the portrayal of the King of Cups, one can anticipate that you will encounter an individual or your soulmate who will enhance your life by bringing profound love and emotional satisfaction.

The King of Cups also provides counsel, advising the containment of personal difficulties within the realm of your twin flame relationship, refraining from involving third parties. Consider the potential emotional impact upon your significant other if they were made aware of your disclosure of their most confidential secrets and ongoing disputes.

The King of Cups assures you that the sentiments your twin flame or ultimate lover harbors for you are genuine.

The individual whom you are divining the Tarot cards for exhibits a profound sense of loyalty towards you.

Furthermore, the King of Cups symbolizes a deep understanding and resonance between you and your twin flame in relation to your emotions, wishes, and requirements. They possess a strong sense of empathy towards you, even if you are not currently aware of it, and will deliberately put forth effort 14

attempt to understand your perspective – an immensely valuable characteristic for fostering a harmonious and cohesive relationship.

Persuasive Discourse In The Era Of Digital Technology

In our rapidly evolving and interconnected society, one can easily lose sight of the immense impact of direct interpersonal interaction. However, as individuals who have engaged in sincere, earnest discussions are aware, there is an inherent significance in the ability to maintain direct eye contact while exchanging one's innermost thoughts and emotions. When executed proficiently, written communication possesses an exceptional capability to establish profound connections with fellow individuals. The majority of individuals do not typically compose articulate written texts or emails, nonetheless, this hurried replacement for substantial interaction can prove to be challenging.

Texting

It has attained status as one of the prevailing modes of interpersonal communication. Although texting can serve as an effective means of maintaining connections with loved ones, it has the potential to give rise to misinterpretations and disputes. In order to ensure effective communication through your texts, it is imperative to carefully weigh the content as well as the tone being conveyed. Below are a few recommendations for effectively communicating through text messages:

When it comes to the content of your text, be clear and concise. The addressee should possess the capacity to comprehend your intended meaning without having to engage in conjecture or interpretation of your verbiage. It is prudent to refrain from employing abbreviations or colloquial language when communicating with individuals who are not well-acquainted with you.

It is equally significant to take cognizance of the manner in which your text is expressed. Emojis and the use of expressive language frequently have a greater capacity to convey the intended tone compared to the literal words employed. To illustrate, if your intention is to convey a playful or amicable tone, incorporating additional emojis and exclamation points into your text can be effective. An appropriately utilized emoji or humorous GIF can imbue your textual messages with a touch of individuality and introduce an element of lightheartedness, should you perceive such an addition to be necessary.

It is advisable to bear in mind that texts are frequently encountered devoid of their original context, thus it is imperative to exercise caution and select your words prudently. In instances where there is uncertainty regarding the interpretation of your written communication by the recipient, it is advisable to exercise prudence and adopt a cautious approach. Be direct. If the statement appears excessively straightforward or lacks emotional depth, consider incorporating a gif or emoji. Please consider the possibility of the recipient misunderstanding your intended message, and therefore, strive to be succinct. When adhering to these principles, text messaging can serve as an effective means of maintaining communication.

Texting and Online Dating

In the context of textual communication, the absence of facial expressions and body language deprives one of the ability to discern the thoughts or emotions of the other party involved. In situations where individuals have yet to have a face-to-face encounter, there exists a lack of informational basis to form assumptions, making it necessary for us to rely on our imaginative faculties in the process of interpreting textual communication. Hence, it is crucial to be mindful of the choice of language and the manner in which your messages are expressed. Exercise extreme caution in identifying any possible instances of miscommunication, and extend the courtesy of assuming the best intentions on the part of the other individual.

Messaging via text can facilitate a deeper understanding of an individual's character and their manner of communication. Additionally, it can serve as an enjoyable method to engage in playful banter, foster a connection, and maintain a fluid exchange of ideas. Leveraging optimistic, uplifting language will facilitate the establishment of a robust rapport with your counterpart. In the event that you require assistance in initiating a dialogue, consider employing open-ended inquiries to prompt your counterpart to divulge further details about themselves.

Although direct interpersonal communication is preferable, it may not be feasible in all situations. The foundation of this mode of communication rests upon the notion that words possess the ability to evoke profound emotional responses in individuals. Put simply, our choice of words can have a discernible impact on the way others perceive us.

"Incorporate these three tactics for enhancing the persuasiveness of your textual content:

1. Transmit optimistic communications: Ensure that the messages you send

convey positivity and a positive outlook. Refrain from negativity, as it will only elicit a negative response from the other individual. For individuals possessing a propensity for employing sarcasm as a form of comedy, it is recommended to reserve such expressions for face-to-face interactions. The use of sarcasm in written communication, particularly in the absence of a prior acquaintance, proves ineffective for conveying one's intended meaning.

2. Employ powerful vocabulary: Exercise caution in your word selection and utilize language that is potent and evocative. Language possesses significant influence, thus it is imperative to exercise prudence in its usage. Exercise caution before transmitting any written communication that may be susceptible to ambiguity, ensuring utmost clarity in your expressions.

3. Utilize proactive language: Refrain from using passive language or expressions such as "I think" or "maybe we could." Opt for active phrases like "I would greatly appreciate visiting that exhibit. Would you consider accompanying me?" or "Why don't we make an attempt at dining at that new restaurant?" Articulating in this manner demonstrates both engagement and determination.

Texting and Romantic Relationships

In contemporary society, it is increasingly common for couples to engage in screen-mediated communication on par with traditional face-to-face interactions. Although the act of messaging can offer a convenient means of maintaining communication, it is not without its share of novel obstacles.

In the realm of interpersonal relationships, it is not uncommon for couples to engage in arguments or prolong tense conversations through the medium of text messaging. Due to the potential for texts to be misinterpreted, there exists the possibility of generating volatile misunderstandings. Moreover, couples may discover that the practice of texting diminishes their capacity to engage in effective communication. When endeavoring to articulate intricate emotions or subjects via written language, it may be effortless for messages to become obscured or misconstrued. Engaging in a prolonged argument that originated from an in-person encounter but carried over into textual communication has the potential to result in unfavorable consequences and ought to be circumvented.

There exists an array of emotional facets in conflict resolution that are incapable of being effectively transmitted via a text message. If you possess a propensity for engaging in fervent textual communication with individuals in your social circle, it would be advisable to reflect upon the number of conflicts that have been successfully resolved through this medium. Any? Alternatively, could engaging in text-based communication regarding this matter serve to protract the discourse until an insurmountable obstacle is encountered, subsequently necessitating the resolution be deferred to a subsequent interaction?

In spite of the obstacles presented by texting, romantic relationships may also garner certain advantages. Text messaging serves as an effective means of maintaining communication with your significant other throughout the course of the day. Furthermore, it serves as a convenient means of communication in instances where verbal conversation or physical meetings may not be feasible. Furthermore, proper utilization of texting can foster feelings of closeness and establish a stronger emotional bond within a romantic partnership.

There are, however, certain instances where the rule does not apply. Certain individuals may find it more conducive to engage in textual communication, as this approach affords them the opportunity to carefully deliberate on their thoughts and expressions without the hindrance of interruptions. This can facilitate more contemplative and profound discourse. In the end, the impact of texting on romantic relationships hinges upon its manner of employment. When employed judiciously and with regard for the desires of one's partner, text messaging can serve as a valuable instrument for fostering intimacy and fostering a sense of connection.

Relationship And Mirroring

Over the years, individuals have excessively complexified the concept of rapport. Extensive volumes have been dedicated to the topic, and establishments offer specialized programs on fostering rapport. The fact of the matter is that establishing rapport can be uncomplicated, as it either exists or doesn't.

This isn't rocket science. Rapport refers to a relational bond or connection that exists between individuals. If there exists mutual affection between you and another individual, a rapport has been established. Consider the initial encounter with an individual. Initially, you may exhibit a certain degree of reservation or aloofness towards that individual. As one spends increasingly more time with them, one's fondness for them grows accordingly. That represents the gradual establishment of rapport." "That signifies the cultivation of rapport over a period of time." "Such is the evolution of rapport over time.

I possess an intrinsic ability to establish rapport swiftly with individuals, rendering me highly adept at fostering likability. Consequently, individuals find it challenging to develop and maintain animosity towards me. In the upcoming chapter, I will delineate the processes I engage in subconsciously, and provide guidance on acquiring the same proficiency.

Matching Perceptions and Pacing

A method I employ to swiftly establish rapport involves aligning my thought patterns with those of the individual in question. Terms such as perceive, sense, and observe are all illustrations of the criteria I seek. These terms illustrate whether an individual operates based on auditory, visual, or kinesthetic stimuli.

Have you ever encountered someone inquiring, 'Do you comprehend the perspective I am presenting?' In response, express understanding with a similar phrase, such as, 'Indeed, I perceive it.' Similarly, when asked, 'Do you comprehend the content of my communication?' a simple affirmation of 'I understand' would suffice. Ultimately, the sensation of being inundated by a multitude of stimuli is profoundly intense. Sensitivity to this experience compels an empathetic acknowledgement of the individual's emotions, necessitating only a simple phrase of comprehension.

As previously mentioned, this concept may appear simplistic, as it indeed is. However, it is important to note that it is highly effective. Just like any other task, the greater frequency with which it is performed will lead to a gradual shift towards unconscious execution. This implies swift connections, increased social connections, and enhanced interpersonal relationships.

The subsequent topic I will address is just as straightforward, namely pacing. Within the realm of hypnosis, there exist terminologies referred to as pacing and leading. They are also applicable for usage in common day-to-day interactions. The majority of individuals incorporate its usage on a daily basis, often without conscious awareness. I possess an exceptional ability to articulate at an impressively rapid pace; my verbal delivery can be likened to traversing at a velocity of 100 miles per hour. It was only when I dedicated myself to the acquisition of effective communication skills that I came to the realization that I should adjust my pace of communication for certain individuals.

We are all acquainted with individuals who possess a propensity for speaking at a languid pace. This individual communicates verbally at an approximate speed of 10 miles per hour. Therefore, when two individuals such as myself, who communicate rapidly akin to the speed of a bullet train, encounter one another, establishing a harmonious rapport becomes a challenging endeavor. Employing the technique of pacing and leading is the most effective approach to resolve this issue.

Pacing and leading refers to the art of initially aligning one's conversational tempo with that of the interlocutor, and subsequently modulating it to shape the desired pace. Suppose you approach an individual who possesses a proclivity for speaking at a leisurely pace. Emulate their decreased pace and gradually commence retrieving items. In due course, it will become apparent that they shall progressively augment their velocity to align with your own. You guide and direct them towards a more optimal pace.

Engaging in this activity is an exemplary method to avoid overburdening the individual. Individuals with a tendency to speak quickly, such as myself, must consciously reduce their pace in order to engage in effective communication with individuals who speak at a slower rate. Similar to the fable of the tortoise and the hare, albeit pertaining to the realm of communication. Adjust your pace to that of the turtle and gradually augment your velocity.

Employ this method at your convenience for the purpose of establishing a connection, diffusing tensions, or effectively influencing an individual. In cases when an individual is agitated and in a highly stimulated mental state, the utilization of pacing and leading techniques can be employed to establish a state of calmness. Do not elevate your anger to their level, rather maintain a slightly lower level of reaction. I am aware that your explanation lacks specificity. Consider it from this perspective: if their intensity level is at a 10, you should align yourself with an 8 or 9. Then continue from there. After reaching the number 8, proceed to descend to 7 and 6 consecutively.

Have you ever engaged in a conversation with an individual who is experiencing mental distress or obsession over a particular matter? Suppose they engaged in a significant dispute with their romantic partner. An instance of employing this method to promote relaxation would involve taking them for a leisurely stroll. Listen to them, but also lower your tone, take on a more relaxed demeanor than them. Your companion will begin to descend and align their speed with yours. It is a common experience that you may have encountered or observed, as it occurs instinctively. Henceforth, you shall remain overtly cognizant of the unfolding events.

The utilization of pacing and leading techniques yields equivalent outcomes. Sales representatives typically exhibit a heightened level of enthusiasm and motivation. Therefore, if the salesman engages in rapid and relentless speech towards a reticent customer, it is highly improbable that the purchase will be made. Their capability lies in decelerating the pace of proceedings, subsequently guiding the prospective buyer towards an equally enthusiastic and favorable state of mind. The probability of a transaction occurring is significantly higher at that juncture.

Exercise #6.1

There are two aspects to address in this exercise. The first step involves becoming attuned to the keywords individuals use to express their typical perspectives on the world. Are their perspectives derived from visual, auditory, or kinesthetic experiences? After attentively hearing their perspective, endeavor to craft a response that aligns with it. This can be achieved by engaging in collaborative practice sessions with a companion. Instruct them to articulate statements adopting a particular viewpoint, and subsequently, address their remarks in accordance with the same viewpoint.

Subsequently, commence focusing on the aspects of pacing and leading. This segment presents a higher level of challenge compared to the preceding portion, but proficiency will be attained with the passage of time. Ensure that you initially align your conversational tempo with that of the other individual. Subsequently, guide your partner in the desired pace. If the individuals exhibit a rapid speaking pace while you maintain a more deliberate speaking pace, make an effort to encourage them to align with your preferred rhythm. Through repeated practice, this will gradually occur instinctively. Persist in your efforts, and you will be astounded by the effortless ease with which this can be achieved when in a state of harmonious connection with another individual.

Mirroring with Body Language

Body language mirroring is widely discussed and prescribed in psychology and NLP literature as the predominant form of mirroring. The underlying principle is straightforward: one should mirror the body language of the individual they aim to establish rapport with. 'Imagine that they are reclining in their chair, with their arms raised and hands gently placed behind their heads.' One may initiate the act of mirroring by reclining in their seat. After approximately fifteen seconds, proceed to elevate your hands and rest them atop your head.

Excessive replication of body language should be avoided when attempting to mirror another person's nonverbal cues. Refrain from mimicking the individual's actions and replicating their physical gestures as they are in motion. This action will severely damage the interpersonal connection, and the individual will perceive you as mentally unstable. In order to circumvent this issue, it is advisable to gradually emulate the movements over a period of time rather than replicating them with complete precision. Similar to the aforementioned example, rather than positioning your hands behind your head, you would place them on the uppermost part. The two occurrences exhibit resemblances, albeit lacking in complete duplication. You also regulate the pace at which you undertake this task.

Time each movement. Exercise a moderate delay of ten to fifteen seconds after their movement, before emulating a similar action. Additionally, approach the task with nonchalance, gradually transitioning into the desired position to create an air of spontaneity rather than contrivance. The greater the degree of naturalness, the lower the probability that the person will perceive it. Over the course of time, individuals are likely to experience a strong sense of connection with you and potentially develop an unconscious inclination to mimic your behavior.

Meetings provide a prime opportunity to witness this phenomenon. While attending classes and participating in meetings at the fire department, I enjoy observing the interpersonal dynamics and identification of individuals who share strong rapport with one another. Upon conducting a swift observation of the room, I discern individuals who exhibit comparable non-verbal cues. Occasionally, I will participate in the observation and interpretation of nonverbal cues with the intention of establishing a subconscious connection with the collective.

An alternate method for gauging the level of rapport you share with someone entails assessing how effectively you align or synchronize with them. The concept in question will be readily recognizable by readers who have experienced military service. Uniformity is a paramount expectation within the military. When soldiers march collectively, they synchronize their steps. This is the reason why in video recordings, a drill sergeant can be heard enumerating the steps as they march. Maintaining synchronization is not solely restricted to the military domain. Companions and relatives will naturally synchronize their footsteps with yours, devoid of any conscious awareness. Whenever my sibling and I are in each other's company, we seamlessly synchronize without conscious recognition thereof.

Respiration serves as an additional indication of a strong rapport established with a person. Now, recognizing this may cause an interruption in your breathing rhythm, based on my personal observations. However, it is worth noting that this phenomenon is quite fascinating. This approach can also be employed to foster rapport, in addition to the previously mentioned methods.

Specific Scenarios For Cultivating Empathetic Communication

For this particular reason, it is recommended for presenters to have a thorough understanding of their audience. There is a considerable number of individuals present in the room, however, it is my belief that their presence does not stem from a random or unbiased selection process. Hence, considering your existing knowledge about your audience, the greater extent to which you can adapt your communication will enhance its efficacy when transmitted. I would dare to assert that there does not exist a singular message or discourse that can be universally applicable to all audiences.

Regardless of the essence of your communication, it is imperative to adapt its various manifestations according to the individuals you encounter and the context in which you find yourself.

Presented here are a series of inquiries regarding your intended audience's perspectives that should be considered when crafting a message that will be publicly imparted, alongside the accompanying instructions for application.

They, who?

They\\\'re there, but why?

What precisely is the motivating factor behind their actions?

What are the predominant cultural or customary regulations governing the specific domain or event (a protest march would exhibit variation compared to a TedTalk)?

With which ideas and vocabulary are they familiar?

What is their deficiency in terms of knowledge?

To what extent can one venture into the realm of peculiarity without disengaging their understanding or connection?

What is the duration of their attention span?

Which images would prove to be advantageous?

What tone, whether authoritative or otherwise, should you assume? Friendly? Storyteller?

What is the level of emotional intensity exhibited by the individuals present in the room? How can you comprehend their emotional perspective?

What tonality is likely to be the most favorably received for different sections?

What is the appropriate manner in which to erect the numerous pieces of material that have been delivered? What should be the tone and content of the initial sentence? What strategies could be employed to effectively elucidate intricate educational resources, particularly those laden with technical terminology? How many articles should it be requisite for you to possess? The number of stories? What is the optimal approach for integrating pathos, ethos, and logos?

To what extent should you omit certain aspects of your discourse due to the diminished level of enthusiasm that your audience typically exhibits compared to your own passion towards the subject matter?

The utilization of empathy in largescale or public discussions will enhance the efficacy of your communication.

Writing

There exists a multitude of approaches to effectively convey your message, encompassing the choice of vocabulary, the organization of words, as well as the integration of visuals and other graphic elements.

Considering the amalgamation of these elements, which combination would most effectively cater to your specific target audience?

You may conveniently employ the identical inquiries utilized in public speaking to enhance the quality of your writing.

Hence, many authors resort to employing titles in the style of clickbait or presenting their work as offering a compendium of seven essential tips to assist individuals in achieving success, happiness, or personal improvement. As those authors possess the understanding that individuals have aspirations for such qualities, although I personally hold a dissenting perspective on the utilization of manipulative empathy, which employs persuasive tactics to achieve desired outcomes (commonly referred to as manipulation, requiring a shrewd and empathetic individual to succeed), it undeniably fulfills their objectives. The aforementioned holds true for the media as well (which elucidates why marketing endeavors yield such success - they wield their influence by strategically catering to your perspective in order to promote their products).

My primary recommendation regarding writing would be to commence by composing that which is crucial for your comprehension. Additionally, ensure that it is composed in a manner that can be comprehended by the intended recipients.

Enhancing the effectiveness of your communication can be achieved by carefully selecting appropriate wording and structuring your thoughts in a manner tailored to the recipient of your message. When engaged in writing, it is important to approach the task with prudence, ensuring that we do not simply transcribe every thought without careful consideration. Certain individuals possess the aptitude to accomplish this task, likely due to their innate ability to understand their audience and access an extensive repertoire of resources. The majority of individuals will often resort to replicating the established conventions of "conventional writing" (such as incorporating anecdotes, visuals, tables, or listicles) that they have been instructed on. However, this approach may not necessarily be the most effective strategy for effectively conveying one's point.

Please be aware that writing also incorporates non-verbal elements. A basic instance of a non-verbal cue occurs when a sentence or a paragraph reaches its conclusion. Furthermore, poetry can provide us with insights regarding suitable imagery in composition, alongside its linguistic aspects.

Ensure that every single component of your composition, encompassing its language, images, narratives, emotions, artistic decisions, and even visuals, duly exemplifies your originality and acknowledgment.

Moreover, it is advised to abstain from employing empathy as a means of manipulation. Enhancing the accessibility of your writing is highly commendable, as is disseminating your acquired knowledge by adapting it to the audience's level of understanding. Nevertheless, employing the context of an audience with the sole intention of establishing a foundation, enhancing one's leadership, or generating sales serves to objectify oneself in the perception of readers and creates a sense of detachment between the speaker and the audience.

Additionally, it illustrates that you are generating something driven by self-centered desires, and that we are simply being used as a tool to achieve your goals.

On Social Media

The manner in which you compose a post will be altered by considering the perspective of your intended audience. It is apparent to everyone that your online conversations primarily reflect self-centered thinking.

In addition, it is improbable that we will peruse any content you publish on the internet. In order to effectively leverage social media for social interactions, it is advisable to engage in dialogue with others rather than speaking directly at them.

I am uncertain as to whether it is necessary to mention this, but expressing one's limited perspective on social media generally does not contribute significantly, as it tends to incite further disputes, quarrelling, and rants that do not effectively aid many individuals, including yourself (aside from a potential sentimental gratification of expressing one's thoughts and appearing to be acknowledged). If that is your desired course of action, engaging in solitary journaling might prove to be more beneficial.

It is imperative that assertive communication be upheld on social media, whereby it is also of utmost importance that:

Furthermore, it is important to note that each network possesses distinctive merits. It is not advisable to disseminate content on Twitter in the same manner as one does on Facebook or Instagram.

The competition for the most valuable assets possessed by individuals, namely awareness, attention, and time, renders message size, immediacy of content, exposure, and pragmatic value as the pivotal attributes of social media. Moreover, it is worth noting that social media platforms are purposely designed to entice users into continuous scrolling, as users are encouraged to focus solely on the content of their choice.

Your content should adequately reflect the competition for these limited resources.

Meetings

I will provide a concise summary (anticipating how empathic communication should shape our meetings). Understanding which inquiries, particulars, or subjects hold the utmost relevance for the individuals present enables you to engage in dynamic conversational exchanges, adapting the discourse accordingly.

Although these meetings may be excellent, there is often a distinct approach that is better suited for professional and organizational contexts.

The agenda for a meeting ought to consider the perspectives and assumptions of all attendees regarding the desired course and outcomes of the meeting, as both parties arrive with certain expectations pertaining to the agenda. Occasionally, the substance may be as uncomplicated as, "We intend to engage in a three-hour conversation," however, to prevent any misunderstandings, ill feelings, or the disconcerting perception that our time was disregarded, an accord must be reached on the subject matter via the empathetic procedure.

It is likely that the duration of your meetings will be reduced due to the implementation of empathy.

Relationships

Empathy should serve as the foundation for interpersonal communication, particularly within relationships. May I kindly request that you inquire of the individual situated across the table:

How can I explain what I want to communicate in the clearest possible terms for their understanding?

What is the recommended seating arrangement during a dispute, preferably in close proximity to each other as opposed to facing one another directly? What is the desired tonality of your vocal expression? Which specific facial expressions, such as nodding, genuine smiling, or mirroring their actions, should you consciously employ, and which ones ought to be consciously avoided?

In the realm of interpersonal connections, it is imperative to duly consider the coexistence of the other individual alongside your own. Effective communication is paramount in a complex relationship, as it is imperative to acknowledge the unspoken agreement that all exchanges should consistently prioritize the well-being of both parties involved. Hence, apart from duly considering the aforementioned matters addressed in this text, it is imperative that you demonstrate a particular concern regarding the impact of the situation on the individual you are engaging with, as well as the necessary adaptations in your communication to align with both of your respective circumstances.

merely generally:

Have you given consideration to the frequency of your correspondence regarding the requirements of the other party?

Alternatively, how you articulate your thoughts?

Alternatively, one could consider the impact of the nonverbal signals emitted during physical proximity between individuals and their influence on the other party.

Alternatively, if certain words hold particular significance for an individual, it is imperative to consider their shared meaning, particularly if they evoke distressing memories. Failing to do so could significantly impair the conversation and undermine the objective of fostering a connection.

In order for any form of communication, regardless of its objective, to yield optimal results, it is imperative to consider the individual's present circumstances. It is imperative that one gains a comprehensive understanding of the perspective, emotions, and lived experiences of others, even when the intention is to provoke them.

Overcoming Unfavorable Habits

Aristotle is widely known for his profound statement: "Our character is a reflection of our habits." This notion holds particular significance in relation to the establishment and perpetuation of behavioral patterns. Developing habits takes time and effort. When specific behavioral tendencies are replicated, they become imprinted within our neural networks. To provide an example, how frequently do you utilize your smartphone for the purpose of reading text messages, browsing through various social media platforms, or making updates to any of your online profiles? Is this behavior driven by deliberate cognitive processes, such as the conscious decision to assess one's Facebook profile, or does it occur automatically, without any specific or conscious intent? It is highly probable that you did not engage in the aforementioned action through deliberate contemplation, but rather due to a spontaneous inclination. This serves as an illustration of a habitual pattern.

Habits can be both good and bad. Certain individuals assist us in progressing, while others impede our advancement. Habits can be cultivated in various domains of life, and communication is no exception. From displaying a propensity for interrupting one's interlocutors to failing to sustain appropriate eye contact, these are a few prevalent negative practices that permeate our everyday dialogues. They exert a substantial impact on our capacity for communication.

Regrettably, the majority of individuals are unaware of their acquisition of inadequate communication practices.

Fortunately, you possess full authority over your habits. You have the ability to liberate yourself from unfavorable habits and substitute them with constructive behaviors. In order to accomplish this, it is imperative to possess a comprehensive understanding of the mechanisms by which habits operate. This chapter aims to provide comprehensive insights into the mechanics of habits, as well as practical guidance on avoiding prevalent negative habits during conversations and implementing effective strategies for improving conversational skills.

How Are Habits Formed?

Have you encountered any subject or skill that has required a substantial amount of time for you to grasp and develop proficiency in? Possibly, it may have taken you some time to acquire the skill of parallel parking. It could have posed an initial challenge, demanding a deliberate exertion of cognitive energy. With consistent application, the task would have gradually become less challenging and more automatic, one could even describe it as habitual. Parallel parking, engaging in physical activity, or engaging in oral hygiene practices are a few illustrations of activities that adhere to a comparable neurobehavioral pattern.

Habits can be categorized as either passive or active. Passive habits arise from the frequent exposure to particular environments, leading to the acclimatization of your body to them. As an example, the physiological responses of individuals engaging in high-altitude climbing involve a gradual acclimatization to diminished oxygen levels. Conversely, certain habits are referred to as active habits due to their establishment through persistent exertion and deliberate action. These are patterns of behavior that can be executed with minimal or no deliberate mental effort. Certain commonplace activities that fall under this category encompass acts such as dental hygiene routines, specifically brushing one's teeth, or even the act of fastening shoelaces. If one is engaged in the act of tying their shoes for the first time, it necessitates deliberate exertion. With continued practice, it will gradually become ingrained and occur reflexively.

Every habit always begins with a psychological pattern known as the habit loop. It entails a three-step procedure. One possible alternative in a more formal tone could be: "The initial facet pertains to a cue or a stimulus." The subsequent phase entails the regular process, while the concluding phase culminates in the incentive. The cue or the trigger effectively prompts the brain to transition into an automatic state, subsequently giving rise to the unfolding behavior. The routine encompasses the actions and conduct in question. It encompasses all aspects that are conventionally associated with the term habit. The ultimate stage culminates in the recompense. The brain finds the outcome favorable, thereby enhancing the recollection of the aforementioned pattern of behavior.

The behaviors involved in habit formation are connected to a cerebral region referred to as the basal ganglia. It assumes a critical function in the facilitation of emotional growth, acquisition and retention of memories, as well as the identification of patterns. The prefrontal cortex, another region of the brain, is accountable for executing cognitive processes related to decision-making. Once a behavior or routine becomes automatic, the decision-making part of the brain is no longer at play and is instead functioning in a sleep mode like state. During this phase, the brain has the capacity to fully disengage while executing the identical task with minimal cognitive exertion or mental resource allocation. Hence, it becomes more convenient to divert one's attention towards alternative tasks while engaging in activities that one is accustomed to. When you establish a consistent routine, be it for brushing your teeth or even driving a vehicle, these actions can be executed effortlessly and without deliberate awareness. It is feasible to engage in cognitive activities and multitask while executing the aforementioned task. This phenomenon is tied to the basal ganglia's capacity to convert a behavior into an inherent, involuntary reaction.

Errors to Steer Clear of During Conversations

Committing errors is exceedingly prevalent. You may be familiar with the adage that states "To err is human." The adage couldn't be more accurate. This principle also extends to instances where errors are made in verbal discourse. It is advisable to endeavor to avoid as many negative habits as one can. Nonetheless, there is no need to exert excessive pressure on oneself to attain flawlessness or perfection during interpersonal communication. It should be noted that one has the ability to enhance any skill or capability they possess through intentional effort, diligent practice, and unwavering consistency. This is the sole matter of importance. Despite any current lack of proficiency, one can always strive for improvement.

Within this section, you will be acquainted with several prevalent negative habits that impede effective discourse. By refraining from indulging in these negative behaviors, one will experience an increased level of ease when engaging in conversations with fellow individuals. There is no need for concern should you commit any or all of these errors. Habits have the potential to be altered at all times. Now, it is incumbent upon us to ascertain any inadvertent errors or undesirable patterns that may have been inculcated over time. Upon gaining knowledge of these obstacles, one can also develop the skills necessary to surmount them.

Examining Your Mobile Device

The majority of individuals habitually direct their attention towards electronic devices such as smartphones, tablets, smartwatches, or any other form of screens. The issue lies in the fact that, within this era of advanced technology, we find ourselves fixated on various electronic displays. As a result, we rarely direct our focus towards others in our vicinity or even observe the current events. To become an adept conversationalist, it is imperative to eradicate a detrimental tendency of failing to fully engage oneself in the given situation. How would you respond if you find yourself engaged in conversation with an individual who demonstrates a lack of willingness to divert their attention away from their mobile device? Alternatively, perhaps they are engaging in aimless perusing of their social media profiles, neglecting to acknowledge your presence even momentarily. It would not elicit a positive emotional response. Indeed, it is highly likely that others will exhibit a similar reaction.

Therefore, it is essential to refrain from incessantly checking your phone while engaged in conversation or seeking to initiate one. Rather, direct your focus towards the speaker. Exhibit attentiveness and strive to be fully engaged in the act of actively listening. When you demonstrate your presence, it inherently signifies your genuine interest in the content of their words. As a result, it becomes more conducive to sustaining an ongoing conversation.

Interrupting

What are your emotions when you are engaged in discourse and it appears that others are not attentive? Maybe you are recounting an exhilarating anecdote, only to be interrupted by someone else just as you were about to conclude it? Alternatively, perhaps you were enthusiastically conveying information and were interrupted by someone who preemptively completed your statement and subsequently went on to express their own thoughts? What will be your emotional response in any of these scenarios? It is highly probable that you will experience a sense of frustration and annoyance, stemming from the fact that you are being disallowed from fully expressing your thoughts.

It is imperative that you bear in mind the aforementioned concept when engaging in discourse with individuals. It can be exceedingly vexing for an individual when they are persistently interrupted or deprived of the opportunity to conclude their narrative. This behavior generally conveys the impression that you lack interest in the perspectives and thoughts of the other individual, indicating a lack of concern. Irrespective of its nature, ensure that you refrain from this behavior. In the event that you become aware of inadvertently interrupting another individual, kindly express your regret and request for them to proceed. I deeply apologize for interrupting you. Please forgive my interruption and kindly continue with your point. Alternatively, "I deeply apologize for interrupting you." Kindly conclude the narrative.

Kindly refrain from monopolizing" "Please avoid monopolizing" "It is advised not to monopolize" "We kindly request you not to monopolize" "Please be mindful not to monopolize" "Exercise fair distribution without monopolizing" "Please ensure equal participation and avoid monopolization" "Resist the temptation to monopolize" "Engage in fair sharing and avoid monopolizing

Make sure that you avoid monopolizing. Did you ever experience situations where it seemed as though the conversation was dominated by a single individual, despite being in a group setting? The issue with individuals who exhibit monopolizing behavior is that they ultimately consume an excessive amount of time that is not proportionate or equitable. Irrespective of the nature of the interaction, be it one-on-one or a group conversation, refrain from monopolizing the discussion. They possess a remarkable skill in diverting the course of any dialogue towards matters concerning their own self or shaping it to suit their preferred narrative. Nevertheless, there may arise situations in which an individual unintentionally dominates the discourse due to their sociable or loquacious tendencies. Or, perhaps they were excited and enthusiastic about what they wanted to share. Regardless of the scenario, it is imperative to refrain from engaging in this behavior.

Bragging

Certain individuals partake in overt and ostentatious self-promotion, while others may prefer the inclination to seamlessly incorporate their selling points into discussions. Enduring the incessant or relentless boasting of another individual is undeniably devoid of enjoyment. To garner admiration or cultivate esteem from others, it is essential to allow your accomplishments to arise organically in the course of conversation. Do not exert undue pressure to introduce the subject matter and refrain from hurriedly persuading others to engage in it.

You should additionally take note of any evident discrepancies among the individuals with whom you are conversing. For example, it is possible that you possess exceptional capabilities in a particular domain, while the individual with whom you are conversing exhibits a heightened sensitivity towards that area. According to your viewpoint, it may appear as an earnest and direct exchange of ideas. Nonetheless, from the standpoint of the recipient, it likely comes across as an act of self-promotion.

In addition, engaging in an ego-driven competition to outdo the other person is equally unappealing. Suppose you were to communicate to someone that you had an enjoyable zip lining encounter during the weekend. The individual asserts that one cannot comprehend the true essence of enjoyment unless they engage in a different pursuit. This exemplifies the tendency to outdo others. Not only does it give the impression of boasting, but it also hinders meaningful conversation. It is important never to fall into the misconception that one should always possess the most noteworthy anecdote or superior experience when engaged in conversation. In a social setting, it is important to bear in mind that there is no necessity for you to be the initial individual to attain the ultimate goal. If an individual seeks your approval, admiration, or exhibits a sense of pride in something, it is appropriate to engage in their delight. Please refrain from attempting to divert attention onto yourself.

Components within a public relations program

When referring to elements, we are discussing the potential components within the public relations arsenal. These factors persist, regardless of whether public relations is managed internally within the organization or outsourced to an external agency.

Several examples include - Noteworthy declarations.

Concise and succinct press releases can be disseminated by the company, addressing various subjects such as the appointment of new executives, facility expansions, establishment of greenfield or brownfield plants, product launches, and inauguration of showrooms, among others.

These occurrences can occasionally lead to brief mentions in relevant publications, as well as occasional coverage in broadcast media. This can result in increased brand recognition and positive word-of-mouth within the target markets.

Important Announcements

Notable advancements such as a significant breakthrough in research and development by the company, the introduction of a groundbreaking new product, and the implementation of a novel corporate growth strategy, representing a prevailing trend within the industry, are among the occurrences that could warrant a significant declaration.

When executed effectively and distributed to the intended recipients, these actions typically lead to the publication of stories in print media spanning from 500 to 800 words, and may frequently attract television coverage from business channels. Occasionally, as part of a significant announcement, there is a deliberate arrangement to complement it with a press conference. The objective of such an occasion is to not only unveil the information but also to exhibit the leadership's perspectives to the media.

"Trend" Press Releases

Trend releases are typically regarded as highly valuable to journalists and the news media, as they enable clients or organizations to cultivate a reputation as an authoritative source of information or a prominent industry influencer. The aforementioned could pertain to the emergence of trends within your particular sector, encapsulating valuable insights that may prove elusive to the general public.

Feature Story Releases

A feature story release possesses newsworthiness, and, of greater significance, demonstrates enduring relevance. It is a task that the media can promptly execute, or a subject that remains relevant enough to be contemplated even after two weeks or even a month. Feature stories can be considered timeless to a certain extent.

In contrast to a conventional news article, a feature presents a distinct perspective or "angle" in media terminology, and it frequently encompasses a significantly greater length compared to a hard news piece covering the same topic.

Video News Releases

One effective approach to visually showcasing a subject is to create background video footage, which aids journalists in conveying the issue through broadcast media.

Several instances could include the dissemination of information regarding the implications of a novel surgical tool, advanced scanning technology, or the implementation of an efficient manufacturing methodology within a sizeable industrial facility.

Webcasts

Webcasts have emerged as a prominent and pivotal public relations instrument in the contemporary landscape.

Individuals are desirous of harnessing the complete range of web and multimedia capacities in order to effectively employ webcasts. This allows for the efficient dissemination of information, leading to a reduction in both time and energy expenditure. Additionally, it fosters an environment conducive to meaningful dialogue between the spokesperson and the media.

Webcasts are an economically viable solution that provides real-time communication to engage with the global media in an immersive and interactive manner, effectively addressing their time-sensitive requirements.

Spokesperson training

Additionally, within this text, we observe the necessity for an organization to have prepared representatives available to engage with the media whenever the situation necessitates it. As a constituent of public relations, it is crucial that spokespersons receive comprehensive training in linguistic proficiency, demeanor, body language, and, most importantly, their ability to communicate effectively and poised in the face of provocation, should such circumstances arise.

In instances where a matter pertaining to a specific domain arises, the media consistently favors engaging with the subject matter experts rather than the designated PR spokesperson. This indicates that the responsibility of facilitating communication with the media extends beyond just the PR contact, but also encompasses individuals in crucial positions.

The PR personnel or team bears the duty to identify a specific group of individuals within the organization and provide them with media training so as to ensure their preparedness for media interactions. This can be achieved through concise sessions that raise awareness among individuals regarding media practices, appropriate terminology for effective communication, as well as general guidelines and restrictions when engaging with the media.

Information source

An organization and its team can play a crucial role in the media landscape by establishing themselves as the primary sources of essential information regarding the industry, emerging trends, technological advancements, and significant market developments, among others. This is accomplished by ensuring prompt availability to key journalists who require information under significant time constraints and pressure to produce news articles.

Informing the media, through both formal and informal channels, that you and your organization are available to provide trend information is an effective method to cultivate strong relationships with prominent figures in the media industry.

Public announcements.

These are commonly employed by charitable organizations for the purpose of disseminating information that is of relevance to the general public. Concise and succinct, these articles are often disseminated by media outlets and broadcasters to provide valuable information to stakeholders of nonprofit organizations.

Op-eds

Opinion editorials are aptly titled as they represent expressed viewpoints in written format, presented in direct contrast to the central editorial section. These articles offer a remarkable prospect to provide comprehensive perspectives, spanning approximately 800 to 1000 words, and have the liberty to offer commentary on various present-day matters. Producing these written pieces and having them published in reputable newspapers significantly enhances the author's credibility and establishes them as a prominent authority in their field. These writings are published under the authorship of these experts and, due to their strategic placement, garner significant attention from a wide audience.

Letters to the Editor

This column is widely regarded as a highly read section within newspapers, and serves as an influential platform to discuss contentious matters, rectify any misunderstandings, or correct inaccuracies related to the company, its products, or services.

Press Conferences

Press conferences serve as a valuable component of the public relations arsenal, although they are often misconstrued in terms of their intended objectives and the appropriate manner in which to conduct them. Public relations professionals should bear in mind and communicate to their clients in advance that it is recommended to engage their services solely for events that hold substantial importance in terms of media coverage.

In a business context, under the current circumstances, these methods would be applicable solely for pressing communication situations such as post-disaster updates or emergency notifications due to shifts in the global landscape, among other similar scenarios.

The media, especially those of high caliber, harbor a distaste for press conferences, as they perceive them as a means of treating information as a commodity, disseminating it uniformly among more than 40 media outlets. There is an absence of a notion of labor or exclusivity, which greatly appeals to accomplished individuals in the media field.

Media Tours

Organizations employ media tours as an additional means to present their facilities to the media.

This used to done physically until now, by inviting select media personnel for a guided tour of the entire operations.

This could potentially occur either at a singular locale or multiple locales, wherein the operations are distributed across.

In contemporary times, owing to technological advancements such as webcasting, video-conferencing, and video news reels, the media is additionally privileged with the provision of virtual tours of the facilities. This includes valuable opportunities for interaction with the senior management, including the Chief Executive Officer of the organization.

Internet based.

The internet has expanded considerably, presenting an extensive array of virtual platforms for public discussions. Along with social media microsites, it provides abundant opportunities to effectively communicate messages, as well as facilitate discussions about organizations, products, and individuals.

Every company is required to develop its own efficient internal systems for monitoring the internet in order to identify suitable opportunities for engagement, tailored to the specific nature of the company's product or service.

Community Meetings

For companies, frequent engagement with the local community is often deemed essential. One effective strategy entails conducting small community gatherings to elucidate initiatives that will have a direct or indirect influence on a specific segment of the population.

Besides an ongoing public relations campaign, active community participation is an essential means to counter the dissemination of inaccurate information, originating from unreliable sources or individuals with vested interests.

Fact Sheets

In cases where an extensive amount of information needs to be conveyed to stakeholders beyond the capacity of conventional press releases, a fact sheet becomes imperative.

Fact sheets encompass historical perspectives, anecdotes, and data while maintaining a well-crafted composition composed of concise sentences focusing primarily on factual information.

Byline or Feature Articles

Byline articles can be employed in various manners - authoring an article for a newspaper, magazine, or online publication possesses a sustained longevity beyond the initial publication date. The byline reprints can be utilized in press kits, dispatched to clients, retained for downloading in the media section of the website, and similar avenues. Bylines serve as one of the most effective means of establishing professional acumen and influence within the industry in which the company operates.

Crafting a byline for media publication entails substantial dedication, as the subjects must be current, captivating for the newspaper's intended readership, and aligned with their editorial schedule.

People-Pleasing

The concept of appeasing others may not sound entirely negative. In light of everything, what is reprehensible about displaying kindness towards individuals and endeavoring to provide assistance or foster their happiness? Individuals who strive to please others are recognized for their unwavering commitment to undertaking any necessary actions in order to ensure the satisfaction of those around them. Although demonstrating kindness and assisting others is generally deemed favorable, excessive efforts to satisfy others may lead to emotional exhaustion, increased stress levels, and heightened anxiety. Individuals who aim to fulfill the expectations and desires of others expend their valuable resources and time, even at the expense of their own needs and well-being. Typically, their actions stem from a diminished sense of self-worth or feelings of insecurity. People-pleasing entails prioritizing the needs of others over one's own. Through a steadfast commitment to prioritizing the well-being of others, individuals who possess people-pleasing tendencies make sacrifices and exert considerable efforts in order to ensure the contentment of those around them.

Numerous individuals who strive to please others often misunderstand people-pleasing as an expression of kindness, driven by their desire to avoid selfishness and uphold a reputation of moral virtue. It is worth noting that those who engage in people-pleasing frequently grapple with prevalent feelings of anxiety, as well as recurrent concerns surrounding issues of control and perfectionism. Their primary objective is to ensure the contentment of all individuals, although this frequently results in them neglecting their own needs and wants.

People-pleasing, at its core, functions as a coping mechanism whereby your preoccupation with others' opinions of you detrimentally affects you, as you strive to obtain external validation and approval. Here are several indications that may suggest that you exhibit behavior characteristic of being excessively concerned with pleasing others:

You consistently acquiesce to attending functions that you have no desire to participate in.

You tend to frequently offer apologies for even the most minor perceived offenses or mistakes.

One might experience feelings of anxiety if subjected to someone's anger.

Individuals have a tendency to involuntarily display laughter in response to the laughter of others, irrespective of their personal assessment of the comedic value of the stimulus that triggered the laughter.

You readily extend assistance to others even amidst demanding commitments.

You exhibit an apparent display of interest, despite being disinterested in the subject matter.

You compromise your principles in order to appease others and subsequently experience remorse.

You consistently demonstrate a deep sense of accountability for the emotional well-being of others.

You consistently refrain from expressing your personal viewpoint. You defer to the preferences of others.

You consistently exhibit a tendency to never decline.

Do any of the foregoing statements resemble your personal characteristics or experiences? If one becomes aware of their long-standing habit of prioritizing others' interests and desires and wishes to make a transformative shift, there exists a promising outlook for such individuals.

Indicators of Being a Person Who Strives to Please Others

Considering the well-being and happiness of others is commendable, however, seeking to appease others may lead to the modification or adaptation of one's conduct and speech with regards to accommodating the reactions and sentiments of others.

You might exert additional effort to ensure the satisfaction of those in your vicinity by making assumptions about their desires and needs. You continually invest your efforts and valuable time in order to engender their approval. This may pose a significant challenge for you in the foreseeable future. If one consistently prioritizes the gratification of others and consistently perceives others' needs and desires as superior to their own, a deleterious impact on one's well-being and interpersonal connections inevitably ensues.

If you remain uncertain regarding whether you are inclined towards pleasing others or simply showcasing an exceptional level of kindness, the following indicators may shed light on your disposition as a people-pleaser:

Your self-perception is marked by a diminished view of your abilities or worth.

The majority of individuals who consistently prioritize the satisfaction of others frequently exhibit diminished self-esteem, deriving their sense of value primarily from the validation bestowed upon them by others. They may hold the belief that their worthiness of love is contingent upon selflessly giving everything to others.

One might hold the belief that individuals only exhibit concern for one's well-being when one is providing value, and that one's self-worth is contingent upon receiving their recognition and accolades.

You Crave Validation

You possess an inherent desire for the approval and acceptance of others. Regardless of whether it concerns individuals with whom you have a strong bond or complete strangers, you find it intolerable when someone holds an unfavorable opinion of you. In order to prevent this outcome, you will go to great lengths to cater to their desires.

For individuals who tend to seek approval from others, there is a significant level of distress associated with the possibility of facing rejection. Fretting over this matter generally induces specific behaviors intended to appease others in order to avoid potential rejection. One might also possess a profound longing to experience a sense of relevance, operating under the belief that they are more likely to receive affection from individuals who rely on their assistance.

One simply cannot refuse

One might express concern that declining a request or offering no assistance could potentially give the impression of one's indifference.

Pursuing their desires consistently appears to be a preferable alternative, even in the absence of willingness or availability on your part to assist. Many individuals who are inclined towards pleasing others tend to consents to tasks that they may not necessarily desire to undertake, such as assisting a friend in the process of relocating. Such patterns can give rise to difficulties as they convey the message that meeting others' needs takes precedence over your own emotions or comfort. There is a possibility that certain individuals may exploit this. They disregard your limitations as they are aware of your tendency to proceed regardless.

You assume responsibility, even in the absence of culpability.

Do you consistently express apologies in situations where something goes amiss? When one possesses a predisposition for accommodating others' preferences, they are readily inclined to assume responsibility, even if the occurrence in question was not of their own doing.

Suppose that your superior has instructed you to arrange for pizza to be delivered for lunch, however, the establishment inaccurately fulfilled the order. Regrettably, the gluten-free pizzas that were specifically requested were inadvertently overlooked, resulting in certain colleagues being unable to partake in the meal. The receipt unambiguously indicated "gluten-free," thus indisputably highlighting the restaurant's error. However, you continue to express apologies repeatedly. You experience a profound sense of distress and hold the belief that your colleagues harbor doubts about your capabilities, undermining their confidence in your competence to fulfill the responsibility of arranging meals.

You hasten to accord consensus, notwithstanding your lack of concurrence.

Being amenable at times can be perceived as an effective approach to garnering approval. Suppose that your colleagues put forth their suggestions for a novel undertaking during a morning session. In professional discourse, one could express the same sentiment as follows: On one occasion, you may convey to a colleague, "That is an impressive notion," while on another occasion, you might assert, "That is an exceptional proposal." It should be noted that these suggestions for the project diverge significantly, and internally, you may not concur with either of them. By acquiescing to circumstances that diverge from your personal convictions merely to maintain harmony, you are inadvertently promoting a cycle of escalating exasperation. When both colleagues' plans display shortcomings, it is incumbent upon you to speak up and inform them, as failing to do so would be detrimental to everyone involved.

You demonstrate difficulties in embodying genuineness.

Adopting a tendency to constantly seek approval from others can impede one's ability to perceive people's true nature. Persistently suppressing your needs will impede your ability to perceive them with clarity, leading to potential uncertainty regarding your desires, and possibly even causing confusion about how to remain authentic to yourself.

It is possible that you may experience difficulty articulating your emotions, despite your desire to do so. Allow me to provide an illustration: One could potentially refrain from communicating to their romantic partner that their actions have caused emotional distress. One might conceive the notion that: "Their intentions were not malicious, therefore expressing my thoughts could potentially cause them distress." This overlooks the reality that their actions indeed had an impact on one's emotional state.

You are excessively generous.

Do you have an inclination towards bestowing generosity upon others? Do you engage in this behavior with the intention of fostering a greater affinity towards yourself from them? The majority of individuals inclined towards pleasing others often exhibit a propensity to offer an excessive amount of support or assistance, resulting in an excessive number of personal sacrifices. Engaging in acts of sacrifice can nourish your sense of identity, yet it also has the potential to foster a sentiment of martyrdom. You are welcome to bestow and continue endowing, imbued with the expectation that others will reciprocate in kind.

No Free Time

Merely having a packed schedule does not necessarily imply that you are inclined towards pleasing others, however, it is essential to thoroughly evaluate how you allocate your leisure time. After attending to your obligations such as childcare, domestic duties, and professional commitments, what remains at your disposal? Is there any time allocated for leisure activities or pursuing personal interests?

Kindly reflect upon the most recent occasion on which you engaged in an activity solely for your personal benefit. Could you contemplate the possibility of multiple instances akin to that? If you are unable to do so, it is possible that you possess a tendency to excessively seek approval from others.

Disputes and Altercations Elicit Distress in You

Individuals who are primarily concerned with satisfying others often experience apprehension towards expressions of anger. This seems pretty logical. When one experiences feelings of anger, it signifies a lack of contentment. Should the primary objective be to ensure the happiness of others and they express anger, it indicates that their satisfaction has not been achieved. To avoid provoking anger, individuals may hasten to apologize or engage in actions aimed at appeasing the other party's emotional state, regardless of whether they are actually irate.

You might experience apprehension towards conflict unrelated to your own involvement. Should you find yourself observing a dispute between two individuals who are acquaintances, it would be prudent to offer them guidance on reconciling their differences, thereby facilitating a resolution to their discord. You may even harbor a covert expectation that they will hold a favorable impression of you for providing assistance.

The Body Language Of Gender

Not all forms of nonverbal communication are universally recognized. There exist disparities in the manner by which individuals communicate. The interpretation of non-verbal cues can often be perplexing when distinguishing between genders. In order to preempt any misunderstandings, it is imperative to grasp the commonly shared indicators as well as the diverse array of cues expressed through individuals' nonverbal communication.

OUTWARD APPEARANCES

An inquiry into external appearances will be conducted in a separate communication. Human beings may possess a collective outer appearance, however, a small number of distinctions exist and are employed for the purpose of differentiation. For example, it is often observed that women tend to exhibit a greater frequency of smiling compared to men. Women frequently smile in order to appear friendly or fulfill social expectations. The connotations associated with smiles are frequently misunderstood. Furthermore, individuals perceive similar external appearances in varying ways. According to a study published by the American Psychological Association, it was found that women were perceived to exhibit more anger and less cheerfulness compared to men, despite having identical external characteristics.

INDIVIDUAL DISTANCES

Individual spatial boundaries and interpersonal distances vary among individuals. Each individual possesses a distinct personal space, representing the amount of physical distance they prefer to maintain in relation to others. However, gender frequently impacts an individual's perception of personal space.

Males: In general, males tend to occupy more physical space than females and utilize larger personal distances. Males display a greater inclination to maintain a physical distance from each other, even in instances where they share a close bond of friendship. Furthermore, they create more substantial areas of cushioning through the utilization of items such as garments, containers, documents, and so forth. Men typically expect that their personal domains be respected and do not respond favorably to intrusion upon their personal space.

Ladies: Women typically maintain more reserved personal spaces when interacting with each other or with male companions. In general, they tend to increase the personal space between themselves and unfamiliar males. Women also create support areas, although they tend to be smaller in size compared to male cushion zones. Women are obligated to retreat when their territories are targeted, and the regions associated with the female cradle are typically disregarded. People are more inclined to handle a woman's handbag than a man's jacket.

The Nonverbal Communication of Women

It is important to take note of subtle variations in female body language that may not be immediately noticeable. Cultural influence plays a role in determining the perception of proper body language. The long-term evolution of female body language exhibits variances that do not apply universally to all women. Nevertheless, numerous women engage in certain fundamental activities in their practical routines.

Body posture and positioning: Numerous women employ closed body language. This behavior may stem from a display of modesty in social contexts. Women, regardless of the situation, will adjust their posture to appear more attractive.

Inclination: Women tend to lean forward when they demonstrate a strong interest in an individual or object. They exhibit a tendency to shift their bodies away when experiencing disappointment or discomfort.

With a smile on our faces, we have just alluded to the requirement for women to exhibit a cheerful demeanor. While it is commonly interpreted as a friendly gesture, averted gaze is generally considered a courteous behavior.

Gaze interaction: Maintaining eye contact signifies attentiveness and a genuine interest, either in the content being shared or the individual speaking. Enrolled pupils serve as an additional testament of keenness.

Contemplating: Women frequently emulate or replicate the actions of each other. On occasion, they will contemplate the nature of mankind.

Lower limbs and lower extremities: The lower limbs and lower extremities often align themselves to accentuate a woman's assets. This incorporates sentimental premium.

Contacting: Women are bound to contact each other than men are.

Tapping: The act of tapping or squirming can be seen as a sign that a woman is experiencing irritation or discomfort.

Four Practical Recommendations For Effective Communication Across Various Platforms

By this juncture, you ought to possess a comprehension of several communication models, the significance of employ strategic approaches in your communicative endeavors, and at present, a paradigm to facilitate the implementation of such strategies.

What remains to be addressed is providing you with guidance on effectively engaging in communication with individuals across various platforms and channels.

The subsequent sections will encompass guidance on effectively conveying your message, encompassing not only the composition of your message but also extending beyond its suitability for a blog platform. This will encompass the composition of an extended feature article, exceeding the length typical of a blog, as well as the development of proficiency in the craft of scripting for video, thereby acquiring an entirely novel aptitude. Video content has gained increasing significance in contemporary times, an aspect I will further delve into during the subsequent social media segment.

Subsequently, I would like to discuss the matter of oral presentations, specifically focusing on the dissemination of scientific knowledge to the general public and strategies for effectively delivering such presentations. I have attended several of these events previously and believe I can offer assistance (please remember that you are already proficient in delivering scientific presentations to scientists, but these techniques will also prove beneficial in this context).

Following this, we shall proceed towards delving into the realm of video engagement techniques and exploring the ways to effectively communicate science through this medium. Subsequently, we will shift our focus to my area of expertise, which lies in leveraging social media platforms for science communication purposes.

The final segment pertains to the importance of timely communication, as observing something that was significant a week ago, during its news cycle, only to find it irrelevant and disregarded at present, is regarded unfavorably.

A consistent pattern that one may observe in the subsequent sections is the abstention from discussing specific particulars. There is a rationale behind this phenomenon and it applies to you as well in terms of your science communication.

The focus of these sections pertains to the concept of communications, rather than intricate specifics. Acquiring the profound skills of effective communication cannot be solely attained through reading literature, yet one can certainly grasp the fundamental principles underlying exceptional communication from scholarly works.

This holds great significance, particularly when you, as a science communicator, are addressing an audience that may not possess expertise in the subject matter. In the limited timeframe available to capture their attention, the focus lies on the concept rather than the specifics.

God is not in the detail, after all, the bible is pretty thin on details.

Mimes Explain My Feelings

Children and adolescents with Asperger's syndrome exhibit considerable challenges in discerning the emotions of others. Often, their apparent lack of concern stems from an inability to recognize these emotions and an even greater difficulty in responding to them promptly.

Hence, it is imperative to diligently cultivate this recognition in order to foster more effective engagement within their surroundings.

The activity involves arranging all the participants of the group into circular formations with the purpose of creating depictions of particular emotional states through the use of modeling techniques.

The child or adolescent with Asperger's Syndrome is considered a key participant. The leader of the group selects an emotion to be portrayed through the medium of mime, subsequently elucidating the entire group regarding the specific situation through the use of a practical demonstration. The selected participant, ASchild, endeavors to make a conjecture.

Individuals may seek insights from their peers and, in light of varying perspectives, endeavor to infer the conveyed emotions.

After successfully identifying the emotion, the individual will be requested to create a representation for the remainder of the group to discern.

In conclusion, a brief contemplation is offered regarding the significance of discerning and empathizing with others' emotions, thereby fostering meaningful interpersonal connections that benefit all involved individuals.

Debunking Misconceptions about OCD

Despite the widespread perception of OCD, there is a lack of comprehensive understanding regarding its true implications. Influenced by depictions observed on social media platforms or in cinematic portrayals, they formulate perceptions regarding the illness. When queried on the nature of OCD as a mental illness, an individual could assert that it predominantly stems from an inherent disposition or a deeply ingrained behavioral pattern. Many individuals tend to make uninformed generalizations and classify every instance of OCD as an inclination to maintain tidiness and organization. While not entirely inaccurate, it fails to accurately depict the disorder and the gravity of its significance within our society. The inclination to maintain things in an orderly manner may be seen as commonplace, yet it should be noted that obsessive-compulsive disorder (OCD) does not simply amount to a preference or desire for neatness. On the contrary, individuals with OCD consider maintaining order as an imperative for their existence. There exists a necessity to fulfill the compulsion for organization and equilibrium. Without a doubt, it is an undeniable compulsion. A person diagnosed with OCD may not be able to function at their best because of recurring intrusive thoughts. They are contemplating whether they inadvertently left the gas supply open, the misalignment of the neckline of the individual they are conversing with, and the appropriate resolution of the issue without appearing peculiar. These thoughts are not as readily dismissed as they were spontaneously arrived. They become immobilized and expand, giving rise to the urge to rectify the issue and provide relief. Listed below are several misconceptions and misguided beliefs pertaining to Obsessive-Compulsive Disorder (OCD).

• Germaphobes:

A regrettable falsehood perpetuated by the media among their extensive and uninformed viewership is the notion that individuals with OCD are characterized solely by excessive handwashing and a fear of germs. Although this statement possesses some truth, it merely touches the surface of the complexities associated with OCD. In order to assuage the unease triggered by concerns of contracting infections or harboring germs, persistent thoughts from which they struggle to escape, individuals resort to engaging in regular handwashing whenever they encounter a surface that their mind perceives as unclean and laden with pathogens. However, this singular symptom of OCD is not exhaustive in its representation, despite the portrayal presented by cartoons, comedies, and Facebook posts. While germaphobia is indeed a manifestation of obsessive-compulsive disorder (OCD) that necessitates serious consideration and should not be trivialized, it is important to acknowledge that OCD encompasses various other expressions that result in equally significant impact on individuals. Individuals with Obsessive-Compulsive Disorder (OCD) may experience an urge to repetitively perform specific actions in order to alleviate their anxiety and restore equilibrium. As we have previously discussed, there are individuals who experience anxiety regarding maintaining eye contact or have a fear of perceiving objects or people in their peripheral vision. For various individuals, it is a struggle against intrusive thoughts, specifically concerning concerns about potentially harboring abnormal sexual inclinations. In succinct terms, it should be noted that germaphobia does not encompass the entirety of obsessive-compulsive disorder (OCD), and not all individuals with OCD display germaphobic tendencies.

Communication - An Innate Human Instinct

Individuals of the human species exhibit inherent sociability. The primary endeavor of each individual is to participate in interpersonal discourse. Through every form of engagement, be it proactive or receptive, we inherently engage in the act of interpersonal communication with fellow individuals. Even our silence implies underlying purpose, which others may decipher according to their own judgement.

The formal alternative to the given statement can be as follows: - The definition of communication, as stated by Wikipedia, is as follows: "Communication, derived from the Latin term commūnicāre, refers to the process of transmitting information through the exchange of concepts, emotions, intentions, attitudes, anticipations, perceptions, or directives, accomplished through various channels such as oral discourse, non-verbal gestures, written text, behavioral patterns, and potentially through other mechanisms such as electromagnetic, chemical, or physical phenomena." It entails the significant interchange of data among multiple participants, be it machines, organisms, or their constituent components.

Although the initial definition is readily comprehensible, the intricacy arises in the subsequent statement, wherein communication is characterized as a 'significant interchange of information'. The long-standing dictum states - "The manner in which one presents information is equally, if not more, important than the information itself." Indeed, irrespective of whether you are delivering a wedding toast, a TED talk, or a momentous speech before a vast audience, it is imperative for your words to have a profound impact. Proficient communication is an indispensable life aptitude and serves as a fundamental cornerstone for achievement in various facets of life. The vast majority of contemporary occupations necessitate proficient communication abilities, rendering individuals who are sociable with enhanced communication skills typically more inclined to foster enhanced interpersonal connections with both friends and family members.

Regardless of whether it is your initial experience or one of many, addressing an audience in various settings, such as delivering a lecture at a university or presenting a school project, can elicit feelings of apprehension even among seasoned professionals, irrespective of their level of preparation. It is, thus, not difficult to envision the predicament faced by novices who undertake the task of addressing a group of people. Nevertheless, despite the widely acknowledged reality that proficient communication ranks among the most crucial aptitudes to acquire and develop in life, it is not often pursued with significant dedication.

What is the technique to guide an individual experiencing a panic attack towards becoming a confident speaker?

Although experience is the most effective approach, by augmenting your self-assurance and familiarity with the fundamentals, you will swiftly succeed in conveying your message.

When observing the televised or public appearances of celebrities, politicians, or business leaders, their apparent composure may raise the question: do exceptional orators acquire their skill through external factors, or is it inherent to their nature? Although it is indeed accurate to say that some individuals possess this innate talent, the vast majority of proficient orators have honed their skills through practical training and experience. They may have undergone formal media training, or acquired their persuasive communication skills through ample exposure to public speaking.

Effective speech is not influenced by the obsolete notion of "elocution," which advocated for a uniform and sanctioned manner of speech. Alternatively, effective public speaking pertains to the ability to articulate oneself confidently and clearly in a public setting. The assurance is derived from a lack of trepidation in being incorrect rather than constantly being correct.

Do not allow apprehension surrounding public speaking to overwhelm you, as this ultimately leads to your presence becoming inconspicuous to the audience, whether it is within a professional setting, your community, or among your loved ones; and I assure you, being unnoticed is a destiny far graver than failure.

Mastering The Art Of Workplace Communication

Engaging in casual conversations holds increased significance within the workplace. Effective communication and proficient conversation skills are vital for successful engagement in business meetings, client meetings, and networking sessions. Devoid of these indispensable competencies, your ideas and diligent efforts will not attain the recognition commensurate with their merit. You needn't search extensively to witness this phenomenon firsthand; a mere glance at the accomplished individuals in your professional sphere, including your superiors and executives, would suffice. Take note of their ability to engage in communication efficiently both amongst themselves and with individuals they may encounter.

Essential Approaches for Mastering Professional Communication in the Workplace

You dedicate a total of forty-five hours per week to your place of employment. This is conceivably the location where the majority of your conscious hours are dedicated, assuming you are engaged in a full-time occupation. Thus, it is in this context that your conversational abilities must truly shine, in order to distinguish yourself from others, capture people's attention, and showcase your capabilities.

1. Actively Seek Feedback

Can you recall the instructions outlined in Chapter Three regarding the necessary steps for developing effective conversational abilities, which necessitate consistent practice? Your colleagues present an optimal opportunity for practicing, as daily interaction necessitates conversation, making it sensible to utilize this time to refine your skills. Commence proactively soliciting feedback from your colleagues subsequent to a discourse you have engaged in with them. Inquire about your performance and solicit their feedback on areas where you can make enhancements. Kindly inform them that you are currently undertaking efforts to enhance your conversational abilities, and they will readily oblige to divulge their thoughts. Additionally, this will facilitate the enhancement of your interpersonal rapport, as you progressively cultivate a wider array of conversational topics.

2. Develop a Sense of Curiosity and Inquisitiveness

Strive to assume the role of an individual who displays a keen interest in the happenings within the professional environment. This will assist you in formulating appropriate inquiries to pose during a dialogue. The greater your inquisitiveness concerning your environment, the greater the abundance of information you will discover that can be utilized effectively with individuals across various professional settings. Furthermore, you will develop a genuine propensity to seek further information about the individuals with whom you engage in conversation, thereby engendering substantive inquiries and fostering constructive exchanges.

3. Enhance Your Demeanor

What is the appearance of your personal image when engaging in conversation with someone? Do you maintain an upright posture, with your shoulders drawn back, exuding self-assurance and accompanied by a cheerful countenance? Alternatively, are you situated in a slouched position, with your shoulders huddled inward, exhibiting signs of anxiety as you perpetually ponder others' opinions of you? In a professional setting, your demeanor is equally pertinent to your communication proficiency as the actual content of your dialogue. Once again, your body language will exert a greater influence than verbal communication. In order to cultivate adept conversational skills in a professional setting, it is important to adopt the demeanor of accomplished individuals who typically exhibit an inclusive and approachable non-verbal communication style.

4. What is your vocal demeanor?

The workplace is a setting wherein an atmosphere of professionalism is imperative, while simultaneously promoting a cordial and approachable ambiance. While it is possible that you maintain amicable relationships with your coworkers, it is essential to ensure that your interactions adhere to the appropriate standards of professionalism. Abstain from engaging in conversations that may result in adverse consequences. Maintain a strong yet non-confrontational stance by employing appropriate language that remains within the boundaries of professionalism.

5. Practicing Open Communication in Your Interactions

Lack of transparency, particularly in a professional setting, will inevitably result in individuals developing a negative disposition towards you as they perceive you as being untruthful and untrustworthy. Being a proficient participant in discussions entails cultivating a bond of trust with the interlocutor, fostering an environment where they feel at ease engaging in a conversation with you. One can accomplish this by consistently upholding honesty during all of their conversations. Do not embellish your arguments with excessive rhetoric in an effort to seem more captivating. Adhere to the objective details, particularly when collaborating within a group setting. When engaging in casual conversations with your colleagues, it is advisable to maintain transparency by openly sharing both the information you possess and the information you lack. This facilitates the establishment of trust, thus fostering a greater propensity for future engagement.

6. Employ a Brief Intermission Following Every Sentence

The workplace is a setting where individuals are susceptible to experiencing elevated levels of stress, as the demands of consistently meeting deadlines and surpassing client expectations create a fast-paced and demanding atmosphere. Despite the demanding nature of work, it is imperative to maintain composure and assertiveness during informal conversations. You can achieve this by refraining from succumbing to the pressure of hastening your verbal expressions. Do not excessively deliver successive sentences as this leads to a futile conversation if it lacks effectiveness. In the preceding chapters, it was highlighted that hastily presenting information can have adverse consequences as it increases the likelihood of overlooking crucial details during delivery. Being adept at engaging in conversations entails assuming a position of authority over the dialogue, where you possess the ability to imbue it with significance. Despite being in a demanding environment, it is imperative to refrain from hastily delivering your statements. Effective discussions are invariably enhanced when the transmission and reception of messages occur with absolute clarity.

7. Do not allow your emotions to govern your actions.

Occasionally, emotional intensity can escalate, which is comprehensible considering the prevailing stress and numerous demands encountered in the workplace. However, it is noteworthy that accomplished individuals engaged in conversation refrain from engaging in this particular behavior. They do not openly display their emotions, particularly if they are not of a positive or optimistic nature. A proficient interlocutor possesses unwavering command over their cognitive state throughout a discourse. This task requires regular practice, however, it is advisable to remember to center your attention on the rhythm of your breath. Inhale deeply and affirm to yourself that everything is under control, and that you possess the capability to manage any challenges that may arise. Exercise caution and refrain from hastily voicing your immediate thoughts, particularly in contentious circumstances where the probability of conveying inappropriate sentiments is higher. Additionally, please be mindful of your tone of voice and the manner in which you choose to reply.

8. Eliminate any signs of nervousness that you may exhibit.

If you exhibit any specific indications that reveal your anxiousness during interpersonal conversations, it is advisable to eliminate them at this moment. Do you exhibit restlessness during a conversation due to feelings of anxiety? Are you engaging in the act of rhythmically moving your feet or fingers to a significant extent? Do you engage in finger manipulation or display fidgety hand movements while engaged in conversation with others? Do you refrain from making direct eye contact? If you have been culpable of engaging in all of these actions previously, beginning today, kindly make an effort to eliminate these nervous mannerisms from your persona, as they have no place in the reformed version of yourself. Henceforth, exercise mindfulness regarding your bodily presence prior to initiating a conversation. Prior to approaching them, assume an erect posture, retract your shoulder blades, and display a pleasant countenance. Subsequently, proceed towards them with self-assured steps and initiate an introduction, particularly if it is your initial encounter with them. Ensure that you maintain a state of relaxation in your body while engaging in conversation with them, and promptly carry out a deliberate self-assessment to ascertain that you are not resorting to any anxious mannerisms. Mastering this may require a considerable amount of time and dedication, as you strive to attain a level of competence and confidence.

Implementing Visual Approaches For Environmental Organization

The manner in which one organizes varies greatly depending on their individual preferences. People exhibit a spectrum of traits from strict adherence to disorderly tendencies in this particular context. If individuals were to carefully examine their own lives, they would likely be able to recognize a diverse array of strategies that contribute to the organization of their lives, as well as certain elements of flexibility that accommodate occasional disorder. Reflect upon your own operational approach. Do you possess a stack of significant items currently positioned on your kitchen counter or your workstation? Are you able to readily locate your culinary utensils or equipment when they are required? Could you kindly facilitate the retrieval of a piece of correspondence that was delivered to you several months earlier? May I inquire about the whereabouts of your automobile keys? Are you consistently aware of their whereabouts? What specific procedures and regulations have you implemented in your personal and professional surroundings to optimize your productivity and performance?

Have you been observing my actions? I possess a distinctive method of organizing and misplacing items, albeit I consistently maintain awareness of the whereabouts of my car keys. How does this relate to the instruction of my students?

The educational process entails imparting knowledge and facilitating the exploration of systems and tools that can effectively contribute to the development of students' personal management approach. Numerous students diagnosed with autism or other learning difficulties exhibit an inherent inflexibility that governs their adaptive responses to their surroundings. Understanding their need for predictability provides a rationale for the rigidity. Collaborating with the necessity for organization can lead to environmental adjustments that yield reduced inflexibility, heightened comprehension, and enhanced operational ease. As students acquire the skills to effectively utilize the available organizational opportunities, they enhance their efficiency. They hold a favorable disposition towards the structure and organization.

I aspire to provide them with that framework, although it is challenging due to my inherent dissimilarity. I possess a higher degree of spontaneity and a proclivity towards disorganization. Do I have any prospects for the future?

A classroom or living environment can be meticulously arranged to offer ample integrated framework. Striving to achieve that objective is likely to yield advantages for both yourself and the students as you coexist. Completed documents are to be placed inside this designated receptacle. The designated location for that toy is on the shelf, precisely at this specified position. The cups should be placed on the uppermost shelf, while the plates are to be arranged on the lower shelf. Utilizing visual cues to facilitate the organization of the environment will enhance the clarity of the organizational system for all individuals utilizing it. Furthermore, the utilization of visual aids aids in the instruction of modifications that are bound to transpire.

Students who encounter learning challenges typically exhibit a requirement for structure and the implementation of organizational strategies. Backing them in this domain leads to significant enhancements in their overall performance.

It is imperative to instruct students on the importance of extracting information from the visual cues that inherently exist within their surroundings.

Educating students on the ability to discern and skillfully utilize the visual indicators in their surroundings constitutes a vital component of communication instruction. Having the capacity to perceive or interpret these signals does not guarantee the capability to respond suitably to the information communicated. This constitutes the aspect of communication. The ability to interpret these cues independently of their context holds little to no significance. Recognizing these elements and subsequently exhibiting a comprehension of their significance by skillfully applying the obtained information is of paramount importance.

Implementing Environmental organization through the practice of labeling

The world in which we live is replete with visual elements that serve as cues to assist individuals in functioning with utmost efficiency. Bathrooms are labeled. So are exits. Numbers are allocated to both rooms and school buses. Students derive advantages from receiving instruction on the identification of preexisting environmental stimuli. Furthermore, it is possible to aesthetically enrich both home and school settings in order to provide students with an augmented visual experience. The inclusion of labels and markers offers an avenue for increased autonomy beyond what a student may otherwise attain. Try these techniques.

Instruct students on the importance of discerning the existing labels and information present in their surroundings.

There is already a substantial presence of labels. However, it does not necessarily imply that students are aware of their significance or possess knowledge regarding their meaning. It does not imply that students will possess the knowledge to apply the information in practical scenarios. Numerous students require explicit instruction on leveraging environmental aids.

Assign designations to the student's individual areas and possessions.

The predominant methods of identification involve affixing students' names onto coat racks, desks, chairs, mailboxes, lockers, and designated lunch box areas. Students receive assistance when labels are used to identify their lunch boxes, coats, gym attire, and all their personal belongings.

Chapter 1 - Assertiveness: Strategies for Expressing Your Perspective

It is commonly believed that assertiveness is an inherent trait. Nevertheless, individuals have the capacity to cultivate assertiveness. Typically, the conventional interpretation of assertiveness is limited to the alternative behavioral patterns of aggression and submission that emerge as a result of a submissive disposition. Behavioral experts hold the belief that the essence of a positive and productive relationship lies in the act of being assertive. Consequently, there exist various courses that have been developed with the intention of aiding individuals in acquiring this proficiency.

Inadequate proficiency in assertive skills can lead individuals to adopt aggressive or passive communication styles, which in turn can contribute to a strained interpersonal dynamic.

Defining Assertiveness

In more formal language, assertiveness may be defined as the practice of forthright and transparent communication intended to uphold and honor the needs, rights, and emotions of the interlocutor. The majority of the definitions of 'assertiveness' encompass terms such as "self-assurance," "optimism," or "uncompromisingness." In actuality, assertiveness encompasses more than that. Assertiveness does not involve exhibiting dominance, anger, or emotion, nor does it entail imposing one's opinions upon others. It encompasses the capacity to exist without being subjected to fear. It entails the capacity to demonstrate honesty and foster trust.

The Attributes of a Confident and Self-Assured Individual

An individual may be labeled as assertive if he/she exhibits -

• Straightforward or candid

• Adaptable with a comprehensive grasp of the principle of reciprocity

• Capable of having his requirements met while demonstrating regard for the needs of others

- Proficient in defining limits and asserting negative responses when appropriate - Capable of establishing boundaries and declining requests when required - Skilled in delineating boundaries and expressing refusal when deemed necessary - Competent in setting limits and voicing denials as needed - Proficient in determining boundaries and stating rejections when called for

• Capable of recognizing one's own errors.

The Importance of Assertiveness

Being assertive is pivotal to achieving success in various aspects of our lives. In reference to the domain of personal boundaries, the attribute of assertiveness facilitates the facile resolution of issues and the amicable settlement of multiple disagreements. The display of assertiveness leads to the eradication of stress and trepidation. These two elements invariably permeate individuals' personal and professional spheres, manifesting as superiors with high expectations, clients dissatisfied with outcomes, and colleagues displaying a lack of cooperation. In the context of such relationships, individuals typically employ a variety of coping strategies, which may encompass avoidance, conflict, aggression, and manipulation of others. While assertiveness may not achieve resolutions as swiftly as meek compliance or aggressive dominance, it remains a crucial social skill that fosters healthy and constructive human interactions.

Classifying Patterns of Behavior: Origins and Consequences

There exist three primary categories of behavior patterns that fundamentally shape the character of all our relationships and interactions. Passive, aggressive, and assertive behavioral patterns are cultivated throughout our maturation process. Although each of us embarks on our life journey with an assertive behavioral pattern, over time, certain defense mechanisms are cultivated. These strategies are designed to assist individuals in effectively managing potential hazards presented in the context of both passive and aggressive conduct. There exist a number of individuals who are capable of upholding a resolute demeanor in their conduct.

Inception of Assertive Behavior

Individuals display their highest level of assertiveness during infancy, as they possess unwavering trust without any reservations. They demonstrate an absence of restraints when it comes to openly expressing their emotions. Their insatiable thirst for knowledge about the world knows no bounds. As a whole, an infant possesses neither ego nor fear, enabling them to exist wholly in the present moment.

During this period, the cognitive faculties of our brain have not yet fully matured. Consequently, there exists no room for varying interpretations, tension, or even scrutiny. As we mature and approach the age of approximately 2 or 3 years, our cognitive faculties start assimilating the information imparted by individuals in our vicinity, gradually attuning our understanding of moral principles and distinguishing between 'correct' and 'incorrect'. There exists a prescribed collection of behavioral and perceptual guidelines that govern our conduct and interpretation of the world. Punishments typically serve to suppress playfulness and reprimand it as misconduct.

Effects of Assertive Behavior

The ramifications of exhibiting assertive behavior can result in cultivating a lifestyle characterized by a robust sense of personal identity, without imposing one's convictions onto others. Some advantages of adopting an assertive demeanor are -

• They consistently prioritize taking action while considering the rights of others.

• They consistently demonstrate a focus on finding solutions

• They possess an optimistic perspective

• They prioritize the concerns and emotions of others.

• They possess excellent listening skills • They demonstrate proficiency in listening and processing information effectively • They exhibit an aptitude for attentive listening • They have a strong ability to actively listen and comprehend information consistently • They display a keen ear for listening and comprehending material proficiently

Nevertheless, there are several disadvantages to consider as well, such as -

• They may lack interest in providing coaching services for individuals who display nonassertive behavior.

www.ingramcontent.com/pod-product-compliance
Lightning Source LLC
Chambersburg PA
CBHW050233120526
44590CB00016B/2062